Welcome to the Kingdom of Zork!

You are bored. There's nothing on TV except stupid reruns. You wander into your local bookstore and pick up an interesting-looking book entitled "Zork: The Forces of Krill." As usual, you turn to the first page and begin reading.

The book is set in the magical land of Zork, where the evil and powerful warlock Krill is about to conquer the kingdom, and only YOU can save the day! There are trolls, gnomes, lizard warriors, sorcerers, and a giant empire to explore. It looks like this book is good!

Do you choose to save the Kingdom? If so, purchase the book and turn to page 5.

Or do you choose to go home and watch reruns? Turn to the next page.

In front of the TV, your eyelids slowly close. A strange sound fills the room. Suddenly your eyes open; your realize that you have been snoring.

You can't get that Zork book out of your mind, but the book store is already closed.

Think again! Wouldn't it be wise to purchase the book now, and turn to page 7?

And watch for these WHAT-DO-I-DO-NOW BOOKS *available from Tor:*

ZORK: The Forces of Krill
ZORK: The Cavern of Doom

#1
THE FORCES OF KRILL

S. ERIC MERETZKY

TOR

A TOM DOHERTY ASSOCIATES BOOK

Interior illustrations by Paul Van Munching

ZORK is a registered trademark of Infocom, Inc.

A TOR Book

Published by Tom Doherty Associates, 8-10 W. 36th St., New York, New York 10018

First printing, August 1983

ISBN: 0-812 57-975-5

Printed in the United States of America

Distributed by Pinnacle Books, 1430 Broadway, New York, New York 10018

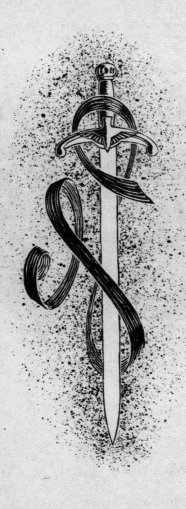

It was a warm, sunny day in early May. June and Bill were going home from school. They were wondering how to spend the afternoon. Should they bicycle to Lookout Pass in the hills outside of town, or explore the deserted fort on the riverbank?

They didn't really want to do either, they realized. The old games, the old explorations —they simply weren't fun or exciting any more. Bill and June discussed this feeling as they passed the unused water station beyond the schoolyard, its high brick walls hidden by a jumble of wild bushes.

Suddenly, June stopped walking.

"What is it?" Bill asked.

"I thought I saw something glowing there, under the bush." June pointed at one particularly thick and twisted bush.

Bill was skeptical, but he followed June to the bush and helped her pull the branches aside. They both saw it at the same time.

"It's . . . it's a sword," gasped June.

"An ancient sword of elvish workmanship," added Bill, "like the one in the story we read in class today!" He reached for the sword.

Turn to page 8.

"Wait!" June cried. "It's a magical sword—
it could be dangerous!"

*Do you think Bill should take the sword? Go to
page 9.*

*Do you think Bill and June should ignore the
sword and continue home? Go to page 13.*

Bill laughs. "Don't be a ninny, June. I won't cut myself!" He reaches deep into the heart of the bush and grasps the haft of the sword.

As he touches the sword, it begins to vibrate wildly. There is a sound like a distant explosion. Immediately, a blinding light flashes from the blade and surrounds June and Bill!

When the light fades and the two startled friends can see again, they realize that they are no longer near the school. They are on a winding path leading down from rocky foothills to a lush forest in a valley below. Behind them, impassable mountains rise, their tallest peaks lost in the clouds above. Their clothes have changed, also. They are now wearing heavy cloth tunics, tied about the waist with wide leather belts. A large leather pouch hangs from Bill's belt. Bill and June stare at each other with mixed excitement and fear.

Suddenly, a group of knights on horseback come galloping around a bend in the trail, heading toward the forest. The leader of the knights, his steed whiter and more powerful than the others, pulls away and approaches.

Turn to page 11.

"Bivotar! Juranda! We feared you were lost to that demon Krill. Ah, you have the sword!" The knight pauses, thinking. "I don't have time to stop—your uncle, Syovar, is meeting us at the campsite. Meet us there—and bring the sword. If you want to know what's happened since you disappeared, you might seek the old man in the village." The tall knight points up the path toward the foothills, then gives a farewell salute and gallops off after the others.

Follow the knights to the campsite? Go to page 14.

Find the old man in the village instead? Go to page 17.

With a last, longing look back at the magical sword, Bill turns away from the hedge. He and June spend the rest of the day watching TV. Spring becomes summer, which passes by without excitement. Eventually, with the leaves beginning to show a hint of yellow, they return to school to begin another year.

THE END

If you stop here, your score is 0 out of a possible 10 points. But you probably deserve another chance.

Go to page 8 and try again.

"Well, Bivotar," Juranda giggles as they walk toward the forest, "I guess it's turning out to be an exciting day after all!"

"I hope we're not getting into trouble, Juranda."

Soon the forest surrounds them, but there is no sign of the knights or the campsite they mentioned. The trees close in overhead, blocking out the light. The forest is damp and quiet, except for the chirping of a distant songbird. The trail narrows, winding so often that Bivotar and Juranda lose all sense of direction.

"I think I smell a campfire!" Bivotar pulls Juranda down the trail. They break out into a deserted clearing, where a dying fire sends a thin finger of smoke up through the treetops.

"There's no one here," says Bivotar.

"Look there." Juranda points across the clearing. There, the trail splits as it leaves the clearing. A signpost stands at the fork. And nailed to the signpost is a handwritten note!

The note reads:

Bivotar, Juranda,
It brings joy to my heart to hear that

Turn to page 16.

you have returned. Sir Ellron tells me that he met you in the foothills and that you have the Sword of Zork. We must hurry off to battle; the armies of Krill are massing again beyond the dam, and I fear they will attack before nightfall. We will go to Ellron's house as soon as possible; meet us there with the sword.

Syovar

Would you take the path to the House of Ellron as Syovar requests? Go to page 24.

Would you take the other path to Aragain Falls? Go to page 26.

Toting the dimly glowing sword, Bill heads up the trail toward the foothills. "Come on, Juranda," he calls back. Soon the two brave adventurers are surrounded by bleak, rolling hills. The few trees that grow here are gnarled and crooked, and clouds cover the sun like a permanent gray stain upon the sky. Juranda shivers and moves closer to Bivotar.

Around a bend in the road, they spot a few huts nestled between the barren hills. As they approach the village, a bearded man emerges from the closest hut. "You escaped!" he cries. He is very old. His long beard is as white as the tall knight's horse, and his face is deeply lined and wrinkled.

"Come in. You must be hungry," he says, entering the hut. The pair follows, their eyes slowly adjusting to the dim interior. As the old man ladles three bowls of stew from a cauldron simmering in the fireplace, he asks, "Have you heard any news since your escape? Things are looking very grim."

Juranda glances at Bivotar and speaks. "Um, actually we haven't heard any news at all. Can you, uh, fill us in?"

Turn to page 19.

The ancient villager's eyes glaze over, as if recalling some dim memory. "Of course you know that your uncle, Syovar, was unable to prevent the fall of the Great Underground Empire. The Empire, under the rule of the Flatheads, controlled every neighboring land, and was the most splendid kingdom in the history of man. But the Flatheads had become decadent, and the forces of Krill had grown so strong that not even a great warrior-wizard like Syovar could stop them.

"Since you were captured by Krill's servants, over two hundred years have passed here in the Land of Frobozz, in the Kingdom of Zork, but Syovar has been unable to overcome the evil that has taken the land. To gain victory, he must have the Sword of Zork, which I see you have rescued. He will also need the Palantirs, the three crystal spheres of legendary power.

"But every day and every year, the forces of Krill grow more daring. No village is safe from their attacks or their spells. The crops no longer grow, and the wind is always cold and sour. Our own village, as you can see, is

Turn to page 20.

deserted now. The men have joined the Knights of Frobozz, and the women and children are hidden away in the mountains." He sighs deeply, then straightens up and stares at them with piercing eyes.

"You, Juranda and Bivotar, must bring the Sword of Zork to your uncle in the forest. The journey will be filled with a hundred terrors and dangers. Remember to avoid the trail of leaves—it leads straight to Krill.

Go to page 21.

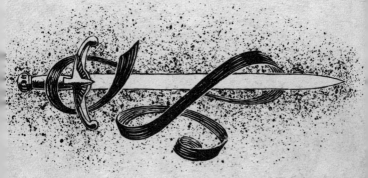

"Of course," he adds, "you could stay here safely with me and hope that the forces of Krill will somehow be driven out of the land."

Would you stay with the old man? Go to page 23.

Would you try to bring the Sword of Zork to the forest? Go to page 14.

Bivotar and Juranda decide to play it safe, and stay with the old man. They learn farming, but their crops are stunted and bitter-tasting. They become hunters, but most animals have already fled the land, and those remaining are so thin they are hardly worth catching.

Occasionally, passing knights bring grim news of yet another defeat by the evil armies of Krill. The nights grow longer, and the wind from the north blows ever colder and more sour. It smells of evil. The Sword of Zork rests safely in a chest in the hut of the old man.

One day, a great darkness covers all. The terrible reign of Krill has been established.

THE END

If you stop here, your score is 1 out of a possible 10 points. But you probably deserve another chance.

Go to page 20 and try again.

Juranda and Bivotar head down the forest trail toward the House of Ellron. The chirping of a songbird comes again, somewhat louder this time. Cheered by the sound and the beauty of these woods, they begin to whistle a cheerful tune, certain that their "uncle" Syovar will defeat the armies of Krill and meet them soon.

The trail suddenly forks again. This time, there is no signpost. One trail is covered with a thick bed of leaves. The other shows the dirt of the forest floor. Next to the fork in the trail stands a large tree. Unlike the other trees in the forest, it has some low branches and could be climbed.

"What do we do now?" asks Juranda.

Take the leaf-covered trail? Go to page 29.

Take the dirt trail? Go to page 32.

Try climbing the tree? Go to page 35.

"I want to see the waterfall," Bivotar says. "Come on."

As they head for Aragain Falls, the trail widens, and the forest begins to thin. In some spots, sunlight filters down to the fern-covered forest floor.

With a startling explosion of noise, a knight on horseback comes charging down the trail from behind them. It is the knight who spoke to them in the foothills, the one that Syovar referred to as Ellron.

"Run!" he cries, as he gallops past. "It's one of Krill's most powerful warlocks! Come this way!" He crashes off down the path in front of them.

Looking back, Bivotar and Juranda see a dark, billowy shape approaching through the trees. "Let's get out of here!" Bivotar cries. Running as fast as they can after the horseman, they break out of the woods at the edge of a wide field. Beyond the field is—nothing. As they watch, Ellron and his steed hurtle over the far edge of the field and vanish.

Their legs aching and their chests pounding, Bivotar and Juranda run to the far edge

Go to page 27.

of the field, and see that a sheer cliff drops hundreds of feet to a mighty river flowing through the canyon below. There is no sign of Ellron anywhere.

Turning, they see a figure entering the field from the forest and walking toward them. Bivotar grasps the haft of the sword, but the approaching figure, a handsome young man

Turn to page 28.

dressed in simple garb, seems both harmless and friendly.

Wait and meet the approaching man? Go to page 41.

Leap off the cliff the way Ellron did? Go to page 37.

"Let's take the leafy path," suggests Bivotar. "Leaves are fun to walk on."

The leaf-covered trail is wide and well-marked at first, but it becomes harder and harder to follow and finally vanishes altogether.

Juranda and Bivotar decide they should turn around and go back, but they discover that they have lost the trail completely. They blunder aimlessly through the forest. The trees become thicker; the light grows dimmer. Strange and sinister noises come from the woods around them.

Bivotar suggests looking for a place to hide. "How about the big pile of leaves, there?" says Juranda, pointing.

As the noises become closer and louder, they tunnel into the pile of leaves. Reaching the center of the pile, they discover a metal grating beneath them. It leads into darkness below. Without warning, the grating swings open, and they fall into the darkness.

An eternity later, Bivotar and Juranda come to rest in a room dimly lit by flickering torches. Before them, sitting on a mighty

Turn to page 31.

throne, is a dark and evil figure. Hatred shines from his blood-red eyes. They can easily guess that this is their enemy, Krill.

"I am glad you have returned," roars Krill with a deep, rumbling laugh. "I must admit, I didn't think recapturing you would be so easy." He approaches Bivotar and plucks the Sword of Zork from his trembling hand. "Thanks for returning this. And now, although you have provided me with a great deal of amusement, I'm afraid you have outlived your usefulness. Guards!"

Tall lizards dressed in battle armor grab them and lead them away toward certain doom. "Perhaps," Bivotar muses, "we should have taken the other trail."

THE END

If you stop here, your score is 2 out of a possible 10 points. But you probably deserve another chance.

Go to page 24 and try again.

"Let's take the dirt path," suggests Bivotar. "It looks safer." Juranda concurs.

They walk along the trail, and soon come to a large clearing in the woods. In the center of the clearing is a white house. Its door and windows are all boarded. On a post near the door is a mailbox.

"Do you think this is Ellron's house?" Bivotar asks.

"Yes! Look, the mailbox says ELLRON."

They walk around the house, looking for a way to enter. The doors and windows all seem tightly sealed. Then, behind the house, Juranda notices that one window is slightly ajar. Bivotar tugs on it with all his strength, and finally it opens just enough for them to enter.

They crawl through the window, and find themselves in a kitchen. On a table are a bottle of water and a long sack smelling of hot peppers.

"I don't know about you, but I'm starved," says Juranda. She opens the sack, and finds a hot-pepper sandwich and a clove of garlic. "Yuk! I'd sure prefer peanut butter and jelly, but I guess it's better than nothing." She gives

Go to page 33.

half of the sandwich to Bivotar, and they share the water. Neither eats the garlic.

"Well, that really hit the spot," Bivotar says. "I hope Syovar gets here soon. Let's look around the house."

The first room they come to is the living room. It is furnished with a heavy wooden trophy case. Inscribed on the case are some ancient runes. They realize, with surprise, that they can read the runes: "Only when the Three Palantirs of Zork are returned to this case can the evil be driven from the land and the Great Underground Empire rise once more." The trophy case is empty. Sitting on top of it is a battery-powered brass lantern. A heavy oriental rug covers the floor.

"We've got to find those spheres and bring them here," says Juranda.

"Sure, but what'll we do in the afternoon?" Bivotar says, laughing.

"Go ahead and laugh. I'm going to look under this rug for a trap door."

Bivotar laughs even harder. "Sure, sure."

Juranda pulls the rug to one side of the room, revealing a trap door. Bivotar's jaw

Turn to page 34.

drops. "Gosh!" he gasps. "How did you know that would be there?"

"I just felt a bump under the rug." She examines the door. "It's locked, but there's a keyhole."

Did you get the bronze key from the bird's nest?

If so, go to page 50.

If not, go to page 53.

"Let's climb the tree, Biv," suggests Juranda. "Maybe we can get a view of the surrounding area."

"Good idea, Juran, but you should do it. You've always been a better tree climber than me."

Juranda agrees and clambers up into the

Turn to page 36.

tree. She climbs as high as she can, but she can't see anything besides the few surrounding trees. However, nestled between two branches is a bird's nest.

"The view's not any better from up here," she calls down to Bivotar. "But there's a bird's nest."

"Who cares? Come on back down."

"Wait . . . I want to look in the nest." She works her way over to the nest and looks inside. There, among the sticks and mud, is a shiny bronze key! She takes the key and climbs back down to the ground.

"Look what I found in the nest!" She shows the key to Bivotar.

"Well, hang on to it. It might turn out to be useful. But we still don't know which path to take."

Take the leaf-covered path? Go to page 29.

Take the dirt path? Go to page 32.

It seems crazy, but Juranda and Bivotar join hands, close their eyes, and leap off the cliff edge after Ellron.

After a heart-stopping moment, they open their eyes and gasp. They are floating slowly down toward the river, as gently as a pair of leaves on an autumn breeze. The view is tremendous. Towering cliffs of white rock rise on either side of the river, and just downstream, breathtaking Aragain Falls thunderously drops its tons of water into the valley below.

Ever so softly, Bivotar and Juranda land on a narrow bank between the river and the cliff. A trail of hoofprints leads upstream along the river bank.

A noise from behind makes them whirl around. An aged hermit, dressed in a tattered robe, is hobbling out of a dark cave in the cliff wall. His scraggly beard reaches almost down to the ground.

"Young lovers, eh?" the hermit inquires.

"Beg pardon?" Bivotar looks puzzled.

"I haven't seen anyone come over Lover's Leap for years. It sure is a lot safer since they installed that Frobozz Magic Anti-Gravity

Turn to page 39.

Field. But I miss picking up all the bones." He cackles strangely.

"Have you seen a knight on horseback go by?" asks Bivotar.

"Eh? Well, I heard some noise out here before you arrived. That's why I came out of my cave. I haven't been out in the sunlight for thirty years . . . or is it forty?" The hermit scratches his head.

"I don't think we've been properly introduced," Juranda points out. "I am Juranda, and this is Bivotar. We're searching for our uncle."

"Bivotar? What the frob kind of name is Bivotar?"

Bivotar shrugs.

"Well, I am called Harlon the Hermit, and I have lived in this cave for nearly eight hundred years."

Juranda and Bivotar must look impressed, because Harlon smiles and continues. "If you are looking for your uncle, perhaps you would like to borrow my boat and sail down the river. It's a very fast way to travel. Of course, some prefer to walk."

Turn to page 40.

"A path leads upstream along the river bank." He points at the trail of hoofprints Bivotar and Juranda noticed earlier.

Take the hermit's boat and travel downstream? Go to page 44.

Go by foot along the river bank path? Go to page 47.

The approaching man waves to them in a friendly fashion, and leaping into a deep canyon seems like certain death, so the two young adventurers decide to wait for him to reach them.

When the man comes near them, Juranda calls out a greeting and begins to introduce herself and Bivotar. But the words freeze in her throat when the handsome young man begins to blur before her eyes. His outline wavers, and his color darkens. Slowly, with a laugh like rolling thunder, the warlock transforms himself into a giant bird of prey, black

Turn to page 43.

as midnight with talons as large as elephant tusks.

Enormous wings, dripping with unwholesome slime, envelop the doomed heroes. Their last sight, before they pass out from the fetid odor of evil in the air, is of tremendous fangs dripping with thick black poison.

THE END

If you stop here, your score is 2 out of a possible 10 points. But you probably deserve another chance.

Go to page 28 and try again.

44

They decide to borrow Harlon's boat, which turns out to be a small rubber raft. "Remember," Harlon says as Juranda and Bivotar board the raft, "this is a magic boat, controlled only by words. Say 'launch' to launch it and 'land' to land it."

Juranda thanks the hermit and cries "Launch!" Sure enough, the raft slides smoothly across the choppy waters and out to the center of the river. The ride is tremendous fun; the river sends a spray of cool mist into their faces, and the current carries the boat along at a fast pace. Rocks poke through the surface of the river, causing rapids which toss the raft about. The magic raft, however, almost seems to steer itself through the rapids.

From ahead, a pounding roar seems to be growing louder. "What's that noise?" Bivotar asks. The current is flowing even faster now.

"Who cares? Isn't this fun?"

Suddenly Bivotar remembers the breathtaking waterfall they saw from the air. "Oh, no! Juranda! The waterfall!"

She stands and sees the river plunging over

Turn to page 46.

the falls. The raft is just seconds away from the edge. "Land! Land!" she cries out. The raft starts to veer toward the shore, but it is too late. They are swept over the falls, plummeting hundreds of feet. Unfortunately, a rubber raft doesn't provide too much protection against the sort of nasty, sharp, pointy rocks that one finds at the bottom of most waterfalls (including this one). The Sword of Zork is lost forever, and so are Bivotar and Juranda.

THE END

If you stop here, your score is 2 out of a possible 10 points. But you probably deserve another chance.

Go to page 40 and try again.

Thanking the hermit, Bivotar and Juranda follow the hoofprints upstream along the river bank. After several miles, the river rounds a bend, and a huge dam comes into view. Water pours over the dam, filling the air with a misty spray.

Within minutes, they reach the very base of the dam. It now towers far above them, a true engineering monument. A zig-zagging staircase climbs the side of the dam. The trail they have been following seems to end at the dam base, where eddying pools form behind the sheet of water coursing over the dam. Also, a passage here leads directly into the cliff wall that lines the river valley. It is dark and silent.

"I say we should explore this dark passage," says Bivotar.

"I think we should try to ford the river in that shallow area at the base of the dam," says Juranda.

"I suggest the stairs to the top of the dam," says an enchanted frog, sitting on a lily pad near the river's edge. "You just might find the Three Palantirs of Zork that will help Syovar overcome the forces of Krill." With a splash,

Turn to page 49.

the enchanted frog leaps from the lily pad and vanishes into the water.

Listen to Bivotar? Go to page 84.

Listen to Juranda? Go to page 86.

Listen to a frog? Go to page 88.

"The key from the bird's nest!" Bivotar says. "Try the key you found in the tree!"

Juranda inserts the key in the lock. It opens easily. The trap door is heavy, though, and the two of them pull with great effort until the door swings open, revealing a rickety staircase leading down into darkness.

"Awfully dark down there," Juranda says nervously.

"Maybe this lantern works." Bivotar turns the lantern on, and it gives off a cheery yellow glow. "Let's go down and have a look around."

They go down the stairs and find themselves in the cellar of the house. On one side, they see the bottom of a metal chute, black with coal dust. It looks very steep and slippery. On the other side, a tunnel leads away from the cellar. Strange, gurgling noises seem to come from the darkness beyond the reach of the lamp.

"This is too spooky, Biv. Let's go back upstairs."

As Juranda starts climbing up, the trap door crashes shut above her. They seem to

Go to page 51.

hear a deep-throated chuckle, but the sound could just be their imagination, or some trick of the underground echoes. A quick check reveals that the trap door is locked and that there is no keyhole on this side! "I guess we might as well see where the tunnel goes."

They follow the tunnel for several minutes. Its walls become rough and uneven. The tunnel turns a corner, and opens into a small underground room carved out of rock. At the far end of the room the tunnel continues. Another passage, dark and sinister, leads off to the left.

Out of the shadows leaps a huge and hairy troll. He is brandishing a bloody axe and blocks the far exit of the room. Bivotar sees a blue glow form around the Sword of Zork, and he feels a powerful energy from it flowing into his arm. Without even thinking, he strikes a fighting pose and approaches the troll. The troll spits out an angry snarl and raises his axe high above his ugly head.

"Biv! This way!" Juranda points to the low, spooky passage to her left. "You'll get killed if you fight that troll!"

Turn to page 52.

Would you escape down the sinister-looking passage? Go to page 56.

Would you fight the troll? Go to page 59.

"Well, we certainly don't have a key," Bivotar points out. "We'll just have to wait around for Ellron or Syovar."

The day has been exciting and tiring, and the two adventurers are soon asleep on the soft living room rug. Some unknown time later, they are awakened by a crash. Ellron enters the living room. Most of his armor is gone, and he is bleeding and stained from battle.

"Quick, to your feet!" he cries. "The forces of Krill have routed our army and have the house surrounded. Syovar has already fled to our underground base. We must escape underground through the trap door."

"But . . . it's locked," Juranda points out.

Ellron manages a chuckle. "Of course, but I naturally have a hidden key. I keep it on a string around the neck of my songbird. The bird and cage are guarded by a spell of invisibility." He waves his hand briefly and recites a strange incantation.

A moment passes, and a tall bird cage appears. Its door is open, and the cage is unoccupied. Ellron's face turns ashen. "The

Turn to page 55.

songbird is gone. Krill's powers are too strong. We are doomed."

A heavy pounding comes from the front door, and the sound of breaking glass can be heard from the direction of the kitchen. The front door splinters apart, and suddenly a horde of lizard-shaped warriors are upon them. Bivotar, Juranda, and the knight are led away in chains. Only doom awaits them.

THE END

If you stop here, your score is 3 out of a possible 10 points. But you probably deserve another chance.

Go to page 24 and try again.

"What am I doing?" screams Bivotar, as the troll rushes at him, the bloody axe twirling above his head. He dodges the troll's charge and ducks into the low passage after Juranda.

They run down the twisting passages together, passing several forks. Finally, with the troll a safe distance behind them, they stop to catch their breath.

"Whew! Thanks, Juranda. I don't know what came over me. It was almost as if the sword was making the decisions for me."

"Well, we're safe now. We just have to figure out how to get out of here."

They soon realize that they're in a maze of twisty little passages, all alike. Every bend and turn looks the same, yet somehow unfamiliar. Deeper and deeper into the heart of the earth they wander. Hunger, thirst, and weariness slow them down. From the darkness nearby come scrambling, scurrying sounds. The noises are frightening and deeply unpleasant.

Time and again Bivotar and Juranda reach dead ends and are forced to turn around and try another passage, always without any hint of progress. They are stumbling with fatigue, and move very slowly. The passages seem to

Go to page 57.

be getting narrower, the light from the lantern seems to be growing dimmer, and the noises from the shadows seem to be getting louder.

Finally, exhausted and terrified, they fall to the ground. With a sputter, the lantern flickers and goes out. Immediately, several

Turn to page 58.

fearsome grues pounce toward them. Grues are horrid creatures whose enormous slavering fangs are the nightmare of every adventurer, and whose only fear is of light. The grues attack Bivotar and Juranda. The rest is too gruesome to describe.

THE END

If you stop here, your score is 4 out of a possible 10 points. But you probably deserve another chance.

Go to page 52 and try again.

Bivotar follows the urging of the sword. As the troll rushes at him, axe first, he jumps aside and swings at the troll, missing by an inch. The troll grunts and swings the axe at Bivotar, who ducks just in time. The axe crashes against the wall, throwing off sparks.

The sword grows warm in Bivotar's hand. With a mighty effort he raises the sword and

Turn to page 60.

swings it in a wide arc toward the troll. The troll seems confused and freezes just long enough to doom himself. The sword sinks deep into the troll, who lets out a wail and expires. His body vanishes in a cloud of billowing black smoke.

"You did it!" shouts Juranda. "I thought you were crazy!"

"It was . . . it was almost as if the sword made the decision to fight the troll. I know it sounds crazy . . ." He scratches his head.

They enter the wide tunnel that exits from the far end of the troll room. It widens and finally opens onto a flat ledge overlooking a vast underground lake below. A steep trail leads down to the water's edge.

Sprawled at the far end of the ledge is the skeleton of a deceased adventurer. Clutched in his bony hand is what appears to be a parchment scroll.

Take the parchment from the skeleton's hand? Go to page 61.

Follow the trail toward the water? Go to page 63.

Juranda approaches the skeleton and snatches the parchment. As she does, the bones collapse in a pile of dust. Juranda jumps back in surprise.

Shaking, she unrolls the parchment. "Look!" she says, "It's a map!" She points to an inscription at the bottom of the map.

Turn to page 62.

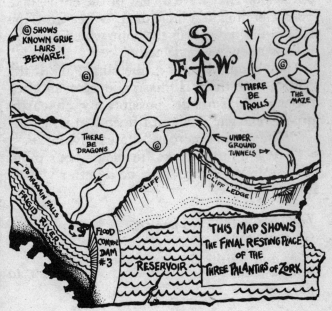

"But it *doesn't* show the 'Final Resting Place,'" says Juranda. "The bottom corner is missing. The Palantirs must be somewhere down there."

"Well, at least it shows the ledge we're on. And see, it indicates that we should go right."

The two adventurers go right, and find a very narrow path leading along the side of the cliff. Soon they have a view of the entire lake below, ending at a huge dam. Water from the lake pours down over the dam, which appears to be somewhat neglected.

They round a bend in the cliff. Part of the path before them is missing, destroyed after the map was made, possibly by an earthquake. The gap is about fifteen feet wide.

"We can jump across," states Bivotar.

"Are you nuts?" asks Juranda. "Let's think for a minute. There must be a better way to get across."

Jump across? Go to page 65.

Wait and think? Go to page 66.

They head toward the lake, taking the steep path leading down from the ledge where the skeleton lies.

The enormous underground lake is lit by phosphorescent mosses growing on the ceiling of the cavern far above. Since the light from the lamp is not needed, they shut it off to

Turn to page 65.

save the battery for future use. The water
stretches off to the north. The far shore is
barely visible through the haze. Every now
and then, air bubbles break the otherwise
calm surface of the water.

A path leads along the hazy shore toward
the east. A distant roar echoes through the
silent cavern from that direction.

"I think we ought to try to swim to the far
shore," says Juranda.

Bivotar is not a good swimmer. He scowls.
"I think we should follow this path along the
shore."

Do you agree with Juranda? Go to page 69.

Do you agree with Bivotar? Go to page 72.

They attempt to jump across the gap and plunge hundreds of feet to sharp boulders at the base of the cliff. This is as unhealthy as it sounds.

THE END

If you stop here, your score is 5 out of a possible 10 points. But you probably deserve another chance.

Go to page 62 and try again.

"I could probably rig up a way to get across if only we had some rope," says Bivotar.

"Do we have anything to build a hot air balloon from?" asks Juranda.

"I don't think so," Bivotar answers, looking around. "I don't have any other ideas, though."

Suddenly, a gnome appears out of thin air. He is dressed in a loud outfit of bright green and orange. "Having some trouble getting across?" he asks.

They nod grimly.

"Well, I can get you across, but it won't be cheap!"

"What do you want?" Bivotar asks, hopefully.

"Hmmm . . . how about that nice sword you're carrying?"

"No!" cries Juranda.

"That belongs to our uncle Syovar!" yells Bivotar.

The gnome is visibly impressed, but says, "Nevertheless, either you give me the sword or you don't get across."

Juranda whispers to Bivotar, "We can't give

Turn to page 68.

up the sword. I say let's go back and try that path down toward the lake.''

"I agree we shouldn't give him the sword,'' says Bivotar, "but hold on a minute. Maybe we can think of some way to trick him.''

Try to trick the gnome? Go to page 75.

Try the path to the lake? Go to page 63.

"Okay," says Bivotar, giving in. "Have it your way." Hooking the sword to his belt, he follows Juranda into the lake.

The water is cool and clear, and after wading through a few clinging plants near the shore their progress is fast and steady.

Turn to page 70.

Without warning, the calm surface of the water is broken by huge slimy tentacles thrusting upward. They lash around and grab the two terrified adventurers. Gripping them tightly, the tentacles drag them underwater, never to be seen again.

THE END

If you stop here, your score is 5 out of a possible 10 points. But you probably deserve another chance.

Go to page 60 and try again.

"Oh, all right, we'll take the path," Juranda says. They begin walking along the shore. It is easy going at first, but the way soon becomes rocky. The distant roaring sound grows louder, and begins to sound like rushing water.

After nearly an hour of walking, Juranda complains. "My feet hurt; let's take a rest."

They stop and sit on some flat rocks near the water's edge. Suddenly they are grabbed from behind and they feel their hands being tied together. A moment later they are turned roughly around, and see two armed lizard-like creatures, standing upright and bearing swords.

Turn to page 74.

"Theesss two will make a fine addition to Krill'zzzz army," one hisses to the other, dribbling saliva down its face.

"Yesss, we'll get a promotion for thisss," hisses the other.

They are led away and forced by a magic spell to join the army of their deadly enemy Krill. Miserably, they fight in battle after battle, living in squalor, losing all hope of ever seeing home again.

THE END

If you stop here, your score is 5 out of a possible 10 points. But you probably deserve another chance.

Go to page 60 and try again.

"Okay, you greedy gnome, you may have the sword, but only when we are on the other side of the gap." Bivotar looks solemnly at the gnome. "Do you agree? Only when we are on the other side of this gap."

"Fine, fine," the gnome agrees, eagerly rubbing his hands together. "Watch this . . . It's one of my best spells."

The gnome begins chanting in some twisted tongue. He waves his arms wildly. His hair flies about his head as if tossed by a fierce wind. Traces of smoke begin to pour from his ears. Suddenly, a sturdy bridge spans the gap. The gnome slumps against the cliff wall, exhausted.

"Hurry across," the gnome urges. "The bridge will last for only thirty seconds!"

Bivotar and Juranda dash across the bridge, with the gnome just behind. When they reach the end of the bridge, they stop and face the gnome, who also stops, but on the bridge several feet from the end. The gnome hoots at them and tells Bivotar to hand him the sword.

"Ah," Bivotar explains, "we agreed to give

Turn to page 77.

you the sword only when we were on the *other* side of the gap. We are now on *this* side, not the *other* side. As you can plainly see, there's *no one* on the *other* side!"

"Whaa?! That's no . . . why you. . ." The gnome looks angry and confused. He leans on the railing of the bridge, and runs a hand through his stringy hair. Then, coming to a decision, he begins rolling up his sleeves. "Well, boy, if you won't give me the sword as we agreed, I guess I'll just have to take it."

Bivotar gulps nervously. The gnome takes a step toward him—and suddenly the bridge vanishes around him. With a look of stunned amazement, he plunges into the abyss, screaming "Frobnooiiiddd!"

"Teach him to be so greedy," Bivotar mumbles as they continue down the trail. "What does the map show now?"

"The path should enter an opening in the cliff somewhere around here," Juranda tells him. Sure enough, a minute later they come to an opening in the cliff wall. They follow the path into this cave. The ground drops steeply, and in many places stairs have been carved in

Turn to page 78.

the rock to make travel easier.

After what seems like hours of following this winding passage, they spot a point of light ahead. It grows larger and larger, and soon they emerge from the tunnel, facing a stunning sight. Towering high above them is a tremendous dam. Water from the reservoir above spills over the top of the ancient and

Go to page 79.

neglected dam. Below them, the spill-off forms a mighty river. Downstream, sunlight pours in from a gaping opening where the river flows out of the underground cavern and into the world of the sun.

"This must be Flood Control Dam Number Three," Juranda says, studying the map. "It's supposed to be the greatest engineering feat in the history of the Great Underground Empire, designed by Lord Dimwit Flathead himself. And that's the Frigid River, there."

With the sound of hoof beats, Ellron the Knight appears, riding toward them along the river bank. He is bloody and disheveled. He dismounts, looking furious. "What in frob's name are you two doing here?"

Bivotar and Juranda look at each other. Finally, Bivotar speaks up. "We were trying to find the Three Palantirs, to return them to the trophy case in your house. We thought we could help. I'm sorry."

Ellron gives a tired chuckle. "Don't be. You both have more courage and cunning than many of my own people, to have gotten this far." He looks more serious. "But finding the

Turn to page 80.

Palantirs is impossible. The map that shows how to find them was stolen over a century ago."

"Is this the map?" Juranda asks, handing the parchment to Ellron.

Ellron looks it over with growing excitement. "Great Fires of Frobizzle! It's the map, all right! How . . . Where did you . . . Never mind. This changes everything. Perhaps . . . perhaps now there's a chance." He thinks for a moment. "Bivotar, Juranda, this is a grave moment. The army of Krill has beaten our knights in battle today. Syovar has fled to our underground base. Those of us still alive are meeting there to form a last defense against Krill. I was taken prisoner, but I escaped just a few minutes ago."

Ellron pauses to arrange his thoughts. "I was heading toward the underground base, but this may be more important. If I can get the three spheres to Syovar before we are completely overwhelmed . . ."

Ellron stops as a beautiful gray owl swoops out of the sky and lands on his shoulder. It

Go to page 81.

holds a paper clutched in one claw. Ellron unfolds the paper. "It is a message from Syovar," he explains, reading.

The knight looks up, his face strained. "Syovar says that Krill's warriors are massing for battle already. If we lose to Krill today, it will be the final defeat. I must go there at once." Ellron puts a hand on each of their shoulders. "You two have already done a valiant job. But though we may survive Krill's attack today, without the power of the Three Palantirs there is no doubt that Krill will soon be victorious. Continue your quest for the legendary spheres. The map will aid you, and the Sword of Zork will protect you. And if you are successful, bring the Palantirs and the Sword to our underground base in the coal mine beyond the dam."

"Count on us, Ellron," says Juranda.

"Right!" adds Bivotar.

"But beware," Ellron cautions, pausing for effect. "Krill may try to trick you. He may even appear in the form of your uncle, Syovar. Just remember that Syovar never removes

Turn to page 82.

the sapphire ring, the Ring of Zork, from which his powers flow." He mounts his white steed. "Good luck, Bivotar, Juranda!" He gallops off.

As Ellron vanishes in the distance, Bivotar says, "No time to waste. Which way now, Juran?"

"This section of the map is incomplete, torn away. But I think . . ." She looks around, then

Go to page 83.

points to a zig-zagging staircase leading up to the side of the dam. "That is the way to the spheres."

Did you get the magic sneakers from the Prince of Kaldorn? If so, go to page 124.

If not, go to page 88.

They enter the dark passage. Within seconds, they are completely surrounded by darkness. Within several more seconds, they are completely surrounded by grues. The grue is a vicious, carnivorous beast whose only fear is of light. They can be found in every dark passage of the Great Underground Empire. They are always hungry. The rest is

too gruesome to describe.

THE END

If you stop here, your score is 5 out of a possible 10 points. But you probably deserve another chance.

Go to page 49 and try again.

They attempt to ford the river at the base of the dam. However, the eddying pools have strong and unpredictable currents. In addition, the water is freezing cold, the river is teeming with all sorts of carnivorous creatures, and sharp boulders lie hidden just beneath the water's surface.

Go to page 87.

When Harlon the Hermit finds their bodies washed up on the river bank many days later, he finds it impossible even to guess how they died.

THE END

If you stop here, your score is 5 out of a possible 10 points. But you probably deserve another chance.

Go to page 49 and try again.

They slowly climb the dizzying stairway. At the top of the dam, the stairs end on top of a small building perched on the dam. The view from here is awesome: the river forming below the dam and flowing out of the cavern; the great reservoir lying in the giant underground cavern behind the dam; the dam itself, ancient but still magnificent.

They enter the small building through an access hatch in its roof. It turns out to be the control room of the dam. Tremendous pipes criss-cross the walls and ceiling.

A control panel with four powerful-looking buttons adorns one wall.

A large window looks out across the surface of the dam itself, where water from the reservoir calmly glides over the top of the dam be-

Go to page 89.

fore plunging into the river valley below. The only exit seems to be a ladder leading up to the access hatch in the roof.

"Let's see what the buttons do," says Bivotar.

"Are you crazy? We'll probably blow ourselves up! Let's cross the top of the dam. The water doesn't look too deep. It'll be safe."

Manipulate the dam controls? Go to page 90.

Leave the controls alone and try to cross the top of the dam? Go to page 94.

Bivotar, feeling slightly nervous, presses the first button. With a faint crackle, the lights in the control room come on. He looks pleased, and jabs at the next button. A loud crashing sound comes from the direction of the dam. "Look!" Juranda cries, standing at the window and looking out.

The floodgates of the dam have opened, and torrents of water are pouring through them. After just a few minutes, the level of the reservoir has dropped enough to stop the flow of water across the top of the dam. In the valley below, the influx of water is swelling the Frigid River beyond its banks.

"Great!" says Bivotar. "Now we can cross the dam in safety." Heady with the success of his first two button-pushings, Bivotar eagerly hits the third button.

Nothing happens for a moment. Then, with a scream, one of the massive pipes bursts open, and rusty, brown water begins pouring out.

"Ooops," says Bivotar.

Water continues spewing from the broken pipe, and within seconds, the water level is up

Turn to page 92.

to their ankles.

"We'd better scram," suggests Bivotar.

At that moment, another pipe bursts, and a large section of wall collapses. The water swirls around their knees.

"Quick, Juranda, out the hatch." He starts

Go to page 93.

toward the ladder. Two more pipes burst, and the water level reaches their waists.

"Look! Look!" Juranda cries, pointing to a hollow area behind the collapsed wall, quickly filling with water. There, resting on a rotting beam, are the Three Palantirs of Zork, glowing with a brilliant light of their own. Immediately, a wash of brown water sweeps over the spheres, and they vanish from sight. The water splashes against their chests.

Try to save the three spheres? Go to page 95.

Or would you try to save your own neck? Go to page 98.

Bivotar and Juranda leave the control room and start crossing the wide dam. The water coursing across the dam tugs at their feet, but they hang onto each other and progress steadily across.

"If we stay here on the reservoir side of the dam," says Bivotar, "we shouldn't have any trouble even if the current gets stronger."

Unfortunately, they step onto a slimy patch of algae and are swept off their feet and over the edge of the dam. The best laid plans . . .

THE END

If you stop here, your score is 6 out of a possible 10 points. But you probably deserve another chance.

Go to page 89 and try again.

Bivotar dives for the submerged Palantirs. The water is murky and filled with powerful eddies, but he gropes around and locates the rotting beam with the three spheres. He places the spheres in the leather pouch hanging from his belt.

He tries to straighten up, but discovers that his leg is wedged between two of the pipes. He cannot work it free. The water swirls far above his head.

Turn to page 96.

Juranda, meanwhile, is treading water; its level has neared the ceiling of the control room. She peers into the muddy water, but can see no sign of Bivotar. Beginning to panic, she dives down to look for him, but only succeeds in banging her head on some submerged pipes.

Just as Bivotar's lungs seem ready to burst, another pipe breaks, loosening the one holding his leg. At that same moment, the window of the control room explodes outwards from the water pressure. Bivotar and Juranda are both swept out of the control room on a wave of muddy water. They land on the surface of the wide dam.

"I thought you were . . ." Juranda sobs and seems embarrassed to be crying, now that the danger is over.

"I've got them," Bivotar gasps between breaths. He points to the bulging pouch.

After Juranda wipes her eyes and wrings out her hair and Bivotar gulps in lungfuls of fresh air, the two intrepid adventurers set out across the dam. The dam's surface is damp and slippery with algae, but eventually they

Go to page 97.

reach the north side, where a path leads upward along a cliff overlooking the reservoir. The cavern ceiling, far above, glows dimly with the light of phosphorescent mosses.

The path soon reaches the entrance to a mine. Huge piles of coal lie heaped around the entrance. Within, they can see flickering torches lining the walls. They enter warily, and almost immediately come to a junction. To their right, the tunnel leads downward into the heart of the mine. To the left is a room which sparkles in the torchlight. They gasp at the sight; treasures and riches of every description are piled up to the ceiling of the room —gold and silver coins fill chests to overflowing.

"Wow!" says Bivotar, his eyes glowing.

Explore the fabulous riches of the treasure room? Go to page 101.

Go directly into the depths of the coal mine? Go to page 103.

"Forget the spheres! Let's get out of here while we can!" Bivotar drags Juranda toward the ladder that leads to the hatch in the roof of the control room. Just as Bivotar steps onto the ladder, another pipe bursts, spraying him with torrents of water and knocking him off the ladder. Dazed, he sinks under the surface of the swirling water.

"Biv!" screams Juranda wildly. She takes a quick gulp of air and dives after him. Groping around the muddy water, Juranda graps Bivotar's tunic and pulls him to the surface. The water is now up to their necks.

"I'm okay," yells Bivotar, gasping. "Get up the ladder." Juranda scrambles up the ladder and out the roof hatch. A moment later, Bivotar emerges. Below them, the window of the control room bursts outward, spraying water and glass across the top of the dam. They drop to the roof of the control room, wet but safe.

So Bivotar and Juranda live to regret Bivotar's selfish decision. Without the power of the Palantirs to stop him, Krill and his armies of slaves and lizard warriors sweep

Turn to page 100.

away the last remnants of resistance. Bivotar, Juranda, Syovar, Ellron, and all the good people of the Great Underground Empire and the Land of Frobozz are enslaved, and the reign of terror and evil lasts a thousand years.

THE END

If you stop here, your score is 7 out of a possible 10 points. But you probably deserve another chance.

Go to page 93 and try again.

Bivotar and Juranda enter the treasure room. The mountains of rubies and emeralds are huge and flawless, and sparkle with reflected torchlight.

A loud noise comes from above. They look up in time to see a huge vampire bat sweeping

Turn to page 102.

down toward them from its perch in the shadowy recesses above. "Fweep! Fweep!" cries the bat. They turn to run, but the bat is upon them, easily lifting one in each claw. The bat flaps its mighty wings and shoots upward, depositing the two frightened adventurers in its nest high above the treasure.

The nest is huge, lined with baubles from below, and filled with the stench of bat guano. The bat climbs onto its perch and apparently goes to sleep, hanging upside down above the nest.

"We've got to get out of here," whispers Juranda. "Aren't bats carnivorous?"

"Trying to climb down from here looks like certain death," counters Bivotar.

Things look bad. Would you remain here at the mercy of the bat? Go to page 107.

Would you try climbing down from the nest? Go to page 108.

Keeping their minds on the more important issue of getting the crystal Palantirs to Syovar, Juranda and Bivotar turn their backs on the treasure and descend into the coal mine.

The tunnels continue downwards, and the torches appear less frequently. Finally, a voice cries out, "Stand and be identified." They stop, and one of the knights steps out of the shadows.

"Oho! It's you two. Syovar will be delighted! Follow me!" He turns and leads them into

Turn to page 104.

a large chamber carved out of the bowels of the coal mine. Many knights are standing and sitting about, eating and poring over maps of the underground. Other knights are sleeping on cots at the far end of the room. The room is lit by many small torches mounted on the wall, casting an eerie glow over everything. One man, taller and better armed than the rest, turns toward them and exclaims, "Yo ho!"

A few broad steps bring him to their side and he embraces them. "This day has proved a happy one after all. Are you well?" They both nod. "Some food for Juranda and Bivotar!" he bellows.

One of the knights ladles out two bowls of lukewarm stew, and breaks off two generous chunks from a loaf of bread. Another knight pulls up a bare wooden bench for them to sit on. Once they are seated and eating, Syovar says, "Ellron tells me that you have the Sword and have been seeking the Three Palantirs. How has the quest gone?"

After they are seated and eating a hearty stew, Syovar says, "Ellron tells me that you have the sword and have been seeking the Three Palantirs. How has the quest gone?"

Turn to page 106.

"We've got them!" Juranda says, smiling.

"Ah! Excellent! We now have a fighting chance to defeat Krill after all." His face hardens. "Well, let's have the spheres and the sword. Time is of the essence." He reaches two massive, bare hands toward them. Something tugs at the back of Bivotar's mind. "Come on, come on," says Syovar, impatiently.

Would you give the Sword of Zork and the Three Palantirs to Syovar? Go to page 109.

If not, go to page 111.

Eventually, the bat awakens. Bivotar and Juranda cower in the corner of the nest. The bat pets them in an almost motherly fashion, and swoops off.

It soon becomes apparent that they have been adopted by the bat as pets and helpers. If they clean the nest well, the bat may bring them some mice or other vermin for dinner. It's a tough life, shoveling bat guano all day and dining on dead rodents. But sometimes, when they've done a particularly good job scrubbing the nest, the bat will scavenge a yummy snake egg for them, and that makes it all seem worthwhile.

THE END

If you stop here, your score is 8 out of a possible 10 points. But you probably deserve another chance.

Go to page 97 and try again.

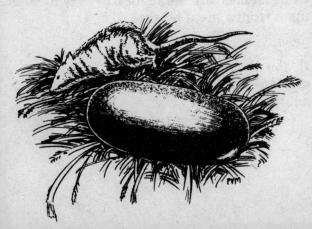

They climb out of the nest and start down the craggy wall, slippery with coal dust, but, as Bivotar predicted, it's certain death. Precious stones are quite deadly when fallen upon from a great height.

THE END

If you stop here, your score is 8 out of a possible 10 points. But you probably deserve another chance.

Go to page 97 and try again.

Bivotar removes the crystal Palantirs from his pouch and hands them to Syovar. He unhooks the heavy sword from his belt and passes it to Syovar as well.

"Thank you, children." He chuckles in an unsettling way, then rises. Before their horrified eyes, Syovar's features blur and a moment later they see standing before them a tall figure draped in black, with blood-red eyes and talons for fingers.

"I am Krill," he bellows. They look around for assistance from the knights, but see that they have all turned into evil-looking armed lizards bearing spears and swords. "Now that you have so graciously given me these sources of incredible power, nothing can stand in my way." Krill waves his bony arm, and he and his lizard warriors are gone in a puff of smoke, leaving Bivotar and Juranda alone in the deserted coal mine to ponder their horrible mistake.

THE END

If you stop here, your score is 8 out of a possible 10 points. But you probably deserve another chance.

Go to page 106 and try again.

"No!" shouts Bivotar, backing away. "Juran . . . he isn't wearing the Ring of Zork! That's not Syovar—it's an imposter."

Syovar curses and spits and then vanishes, to be replaced by an ugly creature, robed in black and radiating evil. The knights have vanished as well, and in their places stand armed lizards, saliva dribbling down their massive jaws.

"Run!" Bivotar cries to Juranda. "Run!"

He dashes back into the passages of the coal mine, Juranda right at his heels. Behind them, a hissing voice bellows, "Capture them!"

They run as fast as they can through the dim and unfamiliar passages. The ground climbs steeply, and their hearts pound from fear and exertion. Close behind their pursuers pound along, their armor clattering. Bivotar stumbles, and Juranda helps him up. The warriors of Krill nearly close the gap between them.

The passages twist and turn, and it is impossible to tell how far they are from the entrance to the mine. Their lungs feel about to burst, but the lizard fighters are still gaining

Turn to page 113.

ground. Bivotar feels a spear graze his leg, and he begins to lose hope.

Around a bend, a large bin of coal sits next to the top of a metal ramp that slopes away into the ground. "Follow me," pants Juranda, hurtling through the mouth of the metal ramp. Bivotar follows, one step ahead of his pursuers.

The ramp is slippery and the two adventurers slide downward at a wild pace. The ramp is also full of sudden twists and turns, making it hard for them to catch their breath. Then, as suddenly as their ride began, it is over, and they land at the bottom in a pile of coal dust.

When their heads clear, they realize that they are in the cellar of a house. Rickety stairs lead up to a trap door, which is open. Voices can be heard from the room above.

Go upstairs? Go to page 114.

Wait here? Go to page 123.

They climb the rickety stairs and find themselves in the living room of Ellron's house. Ellron is there, as are a number of other knights, and someone who looks exactly like the form that Krill took in the coal mine.

"Biv and Juran," he greets them warmly. The caring smile on his face, the kindness in his eyes, and the gentle warmth of his hands on their shoulders, leave little doubt that this is truly Syovar. They do not even need to check the ancient ring that Syovar wears.

"We have the Sword of Zork," says Bivotar, handing it to Syovar.

"And we found the Three Palantirs," adds Juranda, pointing to the bulging pouch.

A look of relief passes across Syovar's face. "Ellron told me of your quest, but when Krill discovered our hideout in the coal mine, and we were forced to flee here, I feared the worst. Now there isn't a moment to lose!"

As if to prove Syovar's last statement, one of the knights, peering through the cracks of a boarded-up window, cries, "Krill's army is surrounding the house! They are easily ten thousand strong."

Turn to page 116.

Quickly, Syovar removes the crystal Palantirs from the leather pouch. They shine with an inner light of their own; the first one fiery red, the second glowing blue like a perfect summer sky, and the third one a shimmering white. He places the spheres in the trophy case, murmuring, "Only when the Three Palantirs of Zork are returned to this case can the evil be driven from the land, and the Great Underground Empire rise once more." He drops to one knee, leaning on the hilt of the Sword, and recites a spell in an unknown tongue.

An arc of light leaps between the three spheres and grows to encompass the entire room. It flashes blindingly bright, and as the light fades, so do their surroundings. The house is gone, and instead they stand on a hill in the center of a vast plain. Before them, like a foul black sea, stand the armies of Krill. Krill himself towers above them, larger than life, a horrible dark cloud before the sun. Behind them, stretching to the horizon, summoned by the power of the Palantirs, stand the legendary Warriors of Zork, clothed in

Go to page 117.

white tunics and shiny battle armor.

"Warriors of Zork!" cries Syovar, now mounted on a mighty steed, his voice carrying with unimaginable power. "I call upon you to rid our kingdom of this scourge. I summon you to remove this blight." His voice rises to a crescendo. "I order you to destroy this evil!" With a cheer that echoes across the plain, the warriors charge forward, engulfing the armies of Krill.

As the battle rages about them, Syovar holds the Sword of Zork high overhead, its brilliant glow like a beacon to the troops. Dark storm clouds form, and lightning streaks down into the heart of the battle. Giant balls of fire plunge overhead and explode into a million tiny infernos. A fierce wind whips across the plain, toppling trees and sweeping horses off their feet.

After an eternity of chaos, it becomes clear that the armies of Krill are losing both ground and strength. The Warriors of Zork press on, seemingly tireless and invincible. With an explosion like thunder, Krill appears, standing before Syovar, his sword drawn.

Turn to page 119.

"Dismount and face my challenge," Krill bellows. Syovar, nodding grimly, leaps from his steed. Steel meets steel, and as the full battle rages about them, Syovar at first seems to be the better swordsman, but Krill uses a variety of tricks and pyrotechnics to distract his opponent. Krill lunges and sinks his blade deep into Syovar's side. The warrior-wizard drops to his knees, clutching at the bleeding wound. Krill raises his sword for a final blow. Bivotar and Juranda gasp, powerless to help.

With a crackle of energy, a blue glow surrounds the Sword of Zork and Syovar's right arm. With surprising strength, Syovar raises the sword and meets Krill's attack. Krill falls back, stunned, and Syovar plunges his blade deep into Krill's heart. Krill clutches at the blade and starts to whisper a powerful curse, but it is too late. He dies, his body disappearing in a giant puff of unwholesome smoke.

A deathly silence falls. Suddenly Bivotar, Juranda, Syovar, and the knights are back in the living room of the house. Syovar lies beside his sword, and Ellron rushes over to attend to his wound. The other knights watch

Turn to page 120.

with concern until Ellron announces that the wound is not serious.

Bivotar and Juranda notice that the crystal Palantirs are now black smoking piles of ash.

Syovar sees their looks. "They have served their purpose and exist no more," he tells them. "They have too much power for one mortal to control; now that the evil has been vanquished, they are best left for the gods." He summons them to his side.

"You have done a great service to me and to everyone in the land. No one can thank you enough." His eyes twinkle knowingly. "I understand you have other places you must be and people you must see." Until this moment, they had forgotten their own lives, but now they realize how terribly they want to go

Go to page 121.

home. "Take this ring," Syovar says, removing the Ring of Zork from his finger. "When you wish to return, and I hope it will not be too long, just place this ring on your finger." He hugs them affectionately, and then incants a brief spell. A puff of gray smoke surrounds them.

Go to page 125.

They wait in the cellar, unsure of what to do. A hissing whine grows louder, and six of the lizard warriors come flying off the ramp, whimpering. They recover quickly, though, and take Bivotar and Juranda prisoner. They are led off, and the warriors confiscate the sword and Palantirs to be used for the evil purposes of Krill.

THE END

If you stop here, your score is 9 out of a possible 10 points. But you probably deserve another chance.

Go to page 113 and try again.

There are no Magic Sneakers and no Princ
of Kaldorn in this book. You have been cheat
ing. Vindictus, the Patron of Decision Novels
appears. Reaching out of the book, he casts
spell on you, and you turn into an unbeliev
ably ugly toad.

THE END

*Your score is negative fifty million billior
zillion points. The score for the best endin,
probably isn't important to a cheater like yor
who probably looks at the last page first.*

They wake, as if from a deep sleep, to find themselves lying in a thicket near the school yard, wearing their regular clothes. They stare at each other in silence.

"Did it really happen . . . or was it just a dream?" June finally asks.

Bill laughs. "I've been trying to get up the nerve to ask you the same question, but I was afraid you'd think I was nuts. I guess we dreamt it all . . ." Suddenly his hand closes on something in his pocket, and he pulls out the Ring of Zork. The light seems to twinkle and dance over its surface. "So it wasn't a dream," whispers Bill.

June points at the school's clock tower. It reads five o'clock. The sun is brushing the tree tops in the west. "Bivotar, look! We're even back in time for dinner. Oh," she adds, lowering her voice a little, "I guess it's Bill again."

"It's Bill now . . . but it will be Bivotar again someday." He smiles at the memory of adventures past and adventures to come.

"And Juranda," adds June, smiling along with him.

Turn to page 126.

They walk slowly home in silence, happily thinking of the many exciting adventures that await them in the Land of Zork.

THE END

Your score is 10 points out of a possible 10 points. Congratulations! You would make a fine adventurer.